The Story
of
Michael Collins

The Story
of
Michael Collins

Iosold Ní Dheirg

FOUNDED IN 1828

GLASNEVIN TRUST

DARDISTOWN   GLASNEVIN   GOLDENBRIDGE
NEWLANDS CROSS   PALMERSTOWN

MERCIER PRESS
IRISH PUBLISHER – IRISH STORY

MERCIER PRESS

Cork

www.mercierpress.ie

First published in hardback by Mercier Press

This edition © Estate of Iosold Ní Dheirg, 2017

© Front cover: Stella Macdonald, 2017

ISBN: 978 1 78117 491 3

10 9 8 7 6 5 4 3 2 1

A CIP record for this title is available from the British Library

In the extracts from other works quoted here we have occasionally altered a word or a phrase where we felt the original would have been beyond the comprehension of the young reader – Editor.

Printed and bound in the EU.

CONTENTS

A WEST CORK BOYHOOD

THOUGH HE WAS only thirty-two years of age when he died, Michael Collins had become in his short life the first Irishman the English feared since Eoghan Rua Ó Néill.

He was born in West Cork, which is not only one of the loveliest parts of Ireland, it is also remarkable for the way in which it has kept its strong Irish traditions. Its people suffered all the horrors of the Great Famine, yet their spirit was unbroken. The slavishness and sense of inferiority only too common in other parts of our country were less evident there. For West Cork was the country of that 'unconquered and unconquerable man', O'Donovan Rossa, whose monument stands today in St Stephen's Green, in Dublin.

The monument to Michael Collins stands beside his mother's home at Sam's Cross, a few miles from Clonakilty. He himself was born nearby at Woodfield (or *Pál Beag* in Irish) on 16 October 1890. His father, Michael, was a man of many talents. A farmer, he was also skilled in building and carpentry. He had received an exceptional education from a hedge-schoolmaster, Diarmuid Ó Súilleabháin, who taught him Greek, Latin, French and Mathematics. He knew both Irish and English, and read all the books he could find.

His wife, Mary O'Brien, bore him eight children, of whom Michael was the youngest – and the pet of the family.

In due course Michael went to school at Lisavaird. The schoolmaster, Denis Lyons, was a forceful personality, and strongly influenced the little boy, who often spoke of him with respect in later years. Lyons, who was a Fenian and a member of the IRB – the Irish Republican Brotherhood – was one of the first to foster the spirit of nationality in Michael.

Of course, there were other people who influenced him, too. The little boy, who excelled at lessons and sport, liked nothing better than to hear tales of olden days from the older people of the district. In particular, there was the local blacksmith, James Santry, himself the son of a smith who had forged pikes for the risings of 1848 and 1867, and whose father before him had been out in 1798. It was in this way that the traditions of Irish nationality were fostered and handed down by word of mouth from generation to generation by an intelligent, though often unlettered, people.

The spread of primary education brought educational benefits. Unfortunately, it had one grave flaw: it tended to destroy what remained of the national language and the national culture. The aim was to make Irish children into law-abiding British citizens, loyal to the British throne. Only the influence of courageous individual teachers combined with parental influence could, and often did, redress the balance.

Next in importance was the influence of books. Fortunately for Michael, all his family were fond of reading, and so he also became a great reader, as can be judged by the fact that at twelve years old he was already studying the writings of Arthur Griffith, the founder of Sinn Féin and a journalist of great ability. Griffith's was the voice to which all that was young and generous in Ireland listened in those days. Little did Michael think that one day he would work with Griffith in the cause of Irish nationality.

When Michael was thirteen years old, it was decided that he should prepare for the entrance examination for the British Postal Service. Many young people from West Cork joined the British civil service each year, having first attended the civil service class in Clonakilty. Michael joined the class and passed the examination for a post boy clerkship. In 1906, when he was fifteen, he went to London, where his sister Johanna was

already working. He took up his first job as a
boy clerk in the Post Office Savings Bank in
West Kensington.

THE GATE OF OPPORTUNITY

Michael Collins was never a person to waste time. In later life, when he had to bear the responsibility for several important posts, he was noted for his efficiency. The foundation had been laid when he was young. Much of his free time was devoted to acquiring useful skills and improving his general education. During his stay in Clonakilty, he taught himself typewriting. He even learned rudimentary sewing, as he believed that even a man should know how to sew on a button!

So it will be seen that working in London had many advantages for him. It enabled him to attend courses which helped to better his position at work. His elder sister Johanna helped him to complete his education, and took a great interest in his study and his work. It was in London also that he met other young Irishmen, many of whom, like

Joe O'Reilly, were to work with him in the cause of Irish freedom.

The Gaelic League and the Gaelic Athletic Association were then flourishing in London as well as in Ireland. Among those associated with the Gaelic League in London in the first ten years of the century were the writers Micheál Breathnach of Cois Fharraige and Pádraic Ó Conaire who, with P. H. Pearse, were to be the founders of the school of modern Irish literature.

It is strange to us today that Michael, whose parents were Irish speakers, had to wait until he went to London before getting an opportunity to learn the language of his ancestors. The deliberate exclusion of the language from the National School programme led a great number of Irishmen to believe that Irish was the language of poverty and backwardness. It is one of the many strange contradictions in Irish history that the rediscovery of the Irish language and its literature by the educated classes took place when it was being discarded in favour of English by the Irish-speaking majority. You could only 'get on' in those days by using the language of the conqueror.

It is rare for the first generation of English-speaking children anywhere to return to the language of their fathers. Michael Collins was an exception in this as in many other ways. He saw that Irishmen worthy of the name should know Irish. That the English conquest of Ireland must be ended was recognised by many of his countrymen; few saw that their English speech set the seal on that conquest.

With his usual thoroughness, Michael started to learn Irish. In later years, his political activities left him little time to perfect his knowledge. He intended to retire to the West Cork Gaeltacht and master the language properly once the war with England was over. Unfortunately, he did not live to do so.

Many Irish boys in London joined the

Gaelic Athletic Association. Michael played both hurling and football. He joined the Geraldine Football and Hurling Club and later became its secretary. His interest in Irish sports lasted all his life.

In 1909 he took the fateful step of joining the IRB. In a very short time he was promoted, becoming treasurer of London and the south of England in 1914. Earlier, he had left the Post Office Savings Bank and secured a position in a firm of stockbrokers, where he remained until 1914. After the outbreak of the First World War, he took up a position in an American firm, the Guaranty Trust Company of New York. The experience of international finance gained during this period was to prove invaluable to him when he became Ireland's first minister of finance.

The assistant manager of the company said of Michael later: 'his duties were simply those of an ordinary bank clerk, but he was recognised as a man of considerable ability. It is conceivable that during his employment with the company he would have many interests outside those by which he earned his daily bread, but if he had, there was no indication of them in his habits and he was never unwilling to do his share of late work, which at this time was continuous. Only on very rare occasions did his sunny smile disappear, and this was usually the result of one of his fellow clerks making some disparaging and, probably, unthinking remark about his beloved Ireland. Then he would look as if he might prove a dangerous enemy.'

For some time, Michael had been thinking of going to America, where better opportunities existed for able and intelligent young men. But when he left, it was to go to Ireland in answer to the call of Seán Mac Diarmada of the IRB, which was now engaged in organising a rising against British rule.

The commissionaire of the Guaranty Trust was an ex-serviceman of the British Army who believed that all men of military age should be at the front, fighting for Britain and the freedom of small nations – Ireland alone excepted. He was delighted when Michael came to say goodbye: 'So you're joining up at last?'

'Yes.'

'The best of British luck to you, my boy,' said the commissionaire.

'Thank you,' said Michael quietly. And he smiled as he walked away, knowing that he was answering the call not of the British king but of *An Sean Bhean Bhocht*.

'THEY GAVE ME OF THEIR BEST'

AT NOON ON Easter Monday, 24 April 1916, the Irish Volunteers and the Citizen Army marched from Liberty Hall to the General Post Office (GPO). At the head of the column were the three leaders: P. H. Pearse, James Connolly and Joseph Plunkett. Just behind marched Plunkett's aide-de-camp, young Michael Collins, a soldierly figure in his staff captain's uniform, tall and light of foot.

The GPO was made the general head-quarters of what was now the army of the Irish Republic. Standing on the steps of the building, Pearse read the Proclamation of the Provisional Government to the People of Ireland. Key buildings in other parts of the city were occupied by other battalions.

Inside the GPO, Collins was busy. Joseph Plunkett, weak and ill, had to rest often in an upstairs room. The efficiency of his aide-de-camp was noticed; otherwise little attention was paid to him. To his comrades, he was simply a member of the garrison, attending to his duties like the rest.

Meanwhile, British troops were being rushed to Dublin to crush the Rising. The centre of the city was completely encircled. By Friday night O'Connell Street was burning. The GPO, bombarded by the British, took fire. The order to evacuate the burning building was given. Michael Collins was one of the group of men who made their escape through smoke and gunfire from the Henry Street door to Moore Street. With them came the leaders, among them the wounded Connolly being borne on a stretcher.

On the following morning, to prevent further bloodshed, the decision to surrender was taken. The Rising was now an accomplished fact. The leaders would die, but their sacrifice would bear fruit.

It was a proud band of men who marched

under a white flag down Moore Street to O'Connell Street where, one by one, they laid down their arms under the eyes of the British Army. The prisoners, both men and women, were marched to the green lawn at the Rotunda Hospital. There they spent Saturday night and part of Sunday herded together in the open, surrounded by a ring of bayonets. On Sunday they were marched to Richmond Barracks and lined up for inspection by the notorious 'G-men' – members of the political division of the Dublin Metropolitan Police – who had been sent to identify the leaders of the Rising. In this they succeeded only too well. Seán Mac Diarmada almost escaped; at the last moment, he was recognised and separated from the other prisoners. With the other leaders, he was court-martialled and executed.

Collins was more fortunate; being un-known, he escaped the attention of the detec-tives. So it was that the young man who, in a few short years was to destroy their intelligence system, slipped unnoticed through their hands, as he was to do many times again. He was removed with about 300 others to a cattle-boat at the North Wall for deportation to England. The Irish prisoners were sent first to Stafford Jail and then to Frongoch, an internment camp in Wales.

FRONGOCH UNIVERSITY

IN FRONGOCH WERE interned all those suspected of Sinn Féin sympathies. No direct evidence had been brought against them. Only a small number had fought in the Rising. Many had taken no part and had been wrongfully imprisoned. Of these, some were sympathisers and some were indifferent or hostile. It was an excellent recruiting ground for those ready to take advantage of it. There were other benefits, too: most of the prisoners were to profit from the exchange of ideas and new bonds of friendship forged at 'Frongoch University', as one commentator called the camp.

As the prisoners included many well-educated and skilled men, it was possible to organise courses in Latin, French, Spanish, Irish, Irish history, book-keeping and shorthand. The Irishmen were much impressed to find that the Welsh workmen who came to do repairs in the camp had kept their own language and always spoke it among themselves. Here was a lesson to be learned by those who dreamt of making Ireland 'not free only, but Gaelic as well'.

Never neglectful of opportunity, Collins worked very hard studying the Irish language and history. At the same time, he used the opportunity provided by internment to draw together the members of the IRB and those of his fellow prisoners who seemed to have the qualities needed for the new army now being formed. A small active minority, determined to renew the fight for freedom, soon made its appearance and provided leadership in the camp. Instruction on military matters was imparted in secret to senior Volunteer officers. Though not a senior officer, Collins characteristically succeeded in getting permission to attend.

Significantly, it was in Frongoch that he first applied himself to getting acquainted with warders, guards, soldiers and others who might be able to do him service. The knowledge thus gained was to be invaluable to him in the days ahead.

The prison authorities now decided to separate those liable to conscription (because of previous residence in England) from the other prisoners. As most of the inmates had never been identified, it proved impossible to find out who was – or was not – liable. Traps were accordingly laid by the authorities to make prisoners identify themselves. Discovery meant removal from the camp to another prison, where those who persisted in refusing to wear a British uniform were imprisoned and ill-treated.

Collins was among the group which urged that all prisoners should stand fast and refuse to identify themselves.

Conditions in the camp were not good. Despite complaints, no improvements were made. When this news reached the outside world, an official of the Home Office was sent to Frongoch to investigate. Collins was one of the delegation of four sent to lay the prisoners' complaints before him. The inventory was long and detailed, and full of figures. The chief cause of complaint was the meagreness and poor quality of the diet.

'And tell me,' said the official wearily, 'is there anything you have enough of?'

'Yes – salt!' came the quick reply.

By December it was evident to the British government that continued internment of Irish prisoners would cause more trouble than it was worth. It was a poor reflection on England's reputation as champion of the freedom of small nations in the eyes of America, at a time when that country's help was badly needed by Britain in the Great War. And so, an order for general release of the Irish prisoners was made on 22 December 1916.

The prisoners were called to a general meeting at which the adjutant of the camp

informed them of the order for their immediate release. He asked the prisoners to
supply names and addresses for travel per-
mits. Suspecting another trick, the prisoners
looked at each other in silence. Suddenly, up
spoke young Michael Collins: 'It's no use –
you'll get no names or addresses from us.'

The adjutant protested that he was not in-
terested in their names and addresses. If they
were afraid of being identified, they could
make out their own lists and hand them to
him. This was agreed.

The internees left Frongoch the next
day. Collins arrived home in Woodfield on
Christmas Day, where he stayed for three
weeks. Then he set off for Dublin, more determined than ever to end British rule in Ireland.

Though none knew it, this unknown young
man already held in his agile brain all the
threads of the network of resistance against
which the might of an empire would not
prevail.

FÁINNE GEAL AN LAE

Dublin had only begun to recover from the shock of the Rising, the execution of the leaders and the mass imprisonment of so many others. Now that some of the prisoners were being released, a new rallying point was needed for all those who would continue the fight.

To aid the dependants of the men of Easter Week, Mrs Tom Clarke founded the Volunteer Dependants' Fund (later the National Aid Association). She needed an energetic, efficient person to act as secretary. Collins, who had helped to reorganise the IRB in Frongoch, now emerged as a leader of the younger men. Mrs Clarke interviewed him. She was most favourably impressed and gave him the post, with the princely salary of two pounds, ten shillings a week. More important still, she confided to him the list of

IRB men given to her by her husband, who foresaw it would be needed if the leaders were killed, imprisoned or otherwise dispersed after the Rising. Mrs Clarke never regretted her decision. As she said later of Collins: 'It gave him the leeway to get ahead and he had the ability and the force, the enthusiasm and drive that very few men had to work on that.'

The same qualities that won him the approval of the rather formidable Mrs Clarke made him the terror of some of his more easy-going associates!

In February 1917 the North Roscommon by-election took place. Supporters of Sinn Féin decided to put forward a candidate in opposition to the Irish Party candidate, Mr Devine. The candidate chosen was Count Plunkett, father of the executed leader and poet, Joseph Plunkett. For Sinn Féin, the hour of destiny had come: would the people of North Roscommon declare for the ideals of Easter Week in the person of Count Plunkett or for the old Irish Party at Westminster in the person of Mr Devine?

Count Plunkett won the election easily. The cause for which his son Joseph had died was now vindicated at the polls. Another victory for Sinn Féin came in the South Longford by-election, which was won by Joseph McGuinness while still a prisoner in Lewes Jail. Later, Éamon de Valera and W. T. Cosgrave were elected in Clare and Kilkenny. The days of the Irish Party at Westminster were numbered.

Meanwhile, the national movement gathered force. The Irish Volunteers were re-formed. Collins was elected to the Volunteer Executive. He organised an information and gun-running system through Sam Maguire, an old acquaintance from his London days. Many Irishmen still worked in the Post Office in London. Sam Maguire went to work and soon had several of those handling the mails working for him.

The British government looked on with dismay at the victories of Sinn Féin candidates, none of whom would take a seat in the Westminster Parliament. Sinn Féin meetings were banned. Several of Collins's co-workers were arrested. Among them was Thomas Ashe, a young Kerryman who had fought bravely at Ashbourne, Co. Meath, during the Easter Rising. He died in prison while on hunger strike as a result of forcible feeding. His funeral oration was given by Collins, following the customary three volleys over the grave. It must have been the shortest speech ever made in Ireland: 'That volley which we have just heard is the only speech which it is proper to make above the grave of a dead Fenian.'

The death of Thomas Ashe – the first to die for Ireland since Easter Week – foreshadowed those that were to come. Perhaps the young orator standing at the graveside of his friend had a premonition that his own life would be forfeit before long.

A DANGEROUS MAN

IN THE SPRING of 1918 Collins was himself arrested. He was accused of making a speech likely to provoke the natives to be disloyal to the crown, and was lodged in Sligo Jail. The First World War was still in progress, and though the tide had turned in England's favour, she was desperately short of fresh troops. So she passed a law requiring Irishmen to join the British Army if called upon to do so. This was known as conscription and it was a mistake on England's part. The results were predictable: all sections of opinion in Ireland united in protest, including the Irish Party, which withdrew from Westminster.

There was much to be done by all Irishmen, both in and out of jail. It seemed to Collins that his place was outside, preparing for the contest of strength between the Irish people and the British government. The Volunteer

Executive ordered him to accept bail; he did so and was released.

The British government decided to discredit the Sinn Féin leaders who were opposing conscription. The means adopted was a 'German plot' in which the Irish leaders were alleged to be involved with the Germans in planning another rising. (No evidence in support of the charge was ever brought forward.) A list of wanted persons was compiled by the authorities. Fortunately, a friendly detective passed on a copy of it to the Volunteers.

Collins carried the warning to the Sinn Féin Executive and the Volunteer Executive. On the following day, over seventy members of Sinn Féin were arrested on charges of complicity. Among them were Éamon de Valera and Arthur Griffith, who had decided to allow themselves to be arrested so as to strengthen Sinn Féin's campaign in the coming election in East Cavan.

Collins was now 'on the run'. He travelled

Dublin on a bicycle and never assumed a disguise. His neat and well-dressed appearance attracted no attention. To Batt O'Connor, he explained: 'I do not allow myself to feel I am on the run. That is my safeguard. It prevents me from acting in a manner likely to arouse suspicion.' It worked perfectly. The police possessed only one poor snapshot – a cause of merriment to his friends. It was published frequently in *Hue and Cry*, the police newspaper. (The description of him ended with the words: 'A dangerous man. Care should be taken that he does not shoot first.') It was not surprising that in these circumstances they failed to recognise their quarry on the occasions they met him.

As director of organisation, Collins had been responsible for drafting a new constitution for the Volunteers. As adjutant-general, he now set about reforming the military organisation. Information was collected from all parts of the country on the Volunteer forces. An inventory of arms and equipment was compiled. Names of the officers and the location of their companies were included. A complete picture of Ireland's resources in men and arms emerged. These left much to be desired. The men needed training; equipment was scarce. Instructors and supplies had to be found. Collins threw himself into the work with his usual vigour, aided by a small staff of devoted helpers.

Much of his activity was devoted to organising the importation of arms and men into Ireland. One of his most trusted agents was an old IRB man in Liverpool named Neill Kerr. Kerr, who worked in a steamship company, had collected arms and ammunition after 1916 and shipped them to Dublin. He was now asked by Michael to take charge of the supply and importation of arms from Liverpool to Dublin, a task he discharged efficiently, and with the help of many courageous sailors on cross-channel boats. This work was carried on up to 1921.

Collins turned his attention to the whole field of communications. The work done for him by Sam Maguire in the British postal service has been described. The network was extended further. Soon, Collins had officials in every major post office in Ireland working for him. Copies of the contents of British government documents were made available to him. Gradually, the communications of the British administration in Ireland were undermined, bringing chaos to Dublin Castle itself.

Even prison walls were no obstacle to communication. The help of friendly warders was enlisted so that it was possible to keep prisoners in Dublin and Belfast informed of all that was happening outside, while they in turn kept their friends informed of conditions inside.

While Collins's chief sources of information were post office workers, detectives, prison warders and seamen, countless individuals everywhere made their contribution:

office workers in the service of the British government, tradesmen, messenger boys, hotel staff, professional people. The resulting communication system was all-embracing and effective. It paralysed Dublin Castle's administration, and greatly helped the establishment and work of Dáil Éireann. For the first time in her long history, Ireland now had 'government of the people, by the people and for the people', to use Abraham Lincoln's definition of true democracy.

One of the most discouraging things in Irish history is the frequency with which risings were brought to nought through the activities of informers, as in 1641, 1798 and 1803, to mention but a few. It was Michael's determination that no informer should be in a position to ferret out the secrets of Dáil Éireann or the Irish Volunteers.

The Royal Irish Constabulary (RIC) was the chief arm of the British administration in Ireland. The members were not policemen in the ordinary sense of the word. They were essentially an armed force whose purpose was to garrison the country for England. Every town and village had its RIC barracks, serving the interests of Dublin Castle. The constables constituted a network of espionage, the extent of which can hardly be realised today. Not only did they spy on the people among whom they lived, they also reported on everything from football matches to meetings in their areas. In country districts especially, the people lived under the eye of the police all the time. A man could not even board a train without it being known to the RIC constable who invariably patrolled the railway station.

The most objectionable thing about the RIC was that its members were recruited from the Irish people themselves to serve the British interest. On the detailed reports sent regularly by the force to Dublin Castle, the whole strength of the British administration reposed. To Michael, it was clear that if the power of the RIC could be broken, the British regime would not survive long.

The first blow against the organisation was struck when President de Valera proposed in Dáil Éireann that the people of Ireland should ostracise the RIC. This measure was agreed upon, and resulted in everyone turning their backs on the police. The people would not talk to them or have any dealings with them whatsoever.

It must be remembered that many men were driven to join the RIC because no other employment was available. It was inevitable that some who did so would grow to hate their work. A member of the detective force in the Dublin headquarters had earlier offered his services to the republicans.

Others followed, risking dire punishment should they be found out. These courageous men became one of Collins's most effective arms against British intelligence. He was to write later:

To paralyse the British machine it was necessary to strike at individuals. Without her spies, England was helpless … Without their police throughout the country, how could they find the man they 'wanted'?

… Spies are not so ready to step into the shoes of their departed confederates as are soldiers to fill the front line in honourable battle. And, even when the new spy stepped into the shoes of the old one, he could not step into the old man's knowledge.

The most potent of these spies were Irishmen enlisted in the British services. Well might every Irishman at present ask himself if we were doing a wrong thing in getting rid of a system which was responsible for bringing these men into the ranks of the opponents of their own race.

One April night, Collins carried out a daring scheme planned with Ned Broy, the friendly detective of the G Division. It was a midnight visit to the detective department of the general police headquarters in Brunswick Street (now Pearse Street), Dublin. The purpose of the visit was to examine the secret reports and documents in the department.

With Seán Nunan, Collins arrived at midnight and was admitted by Broy, who was the officer on duty that night. The other members of the force were sleeping in a dormitory elsewhere in the building. Just as the visitors entered, they heard the sound of breaking glass. A drunken soldier had just broken the glass in one of the front windows. Anxiously, the three men waited until they heard the policeman outside remove the offender.

Broy led them up to a small room on the upper floor in which the secret records were kept. Collins spent several hours going through them and making notes. He found one report on himself which made him laugh. It began: 'He comes from a brainy Cork family.'

When he left police headquarters early that morning, Collins carried in his head all the details of the police network in Ireland. Warnings were sent to the detectives who were spying on members of Sinn Féin. Many heeded the warnings, but those who ignored them paid with their lives. Among those shot was the detective who had helped to send Seán Mac Diarmada to his death in 1916. By a strange coincidence, he was one of the few members of the force who knew Collins's appearance well enough to recognise him.

'STONE WALLS DO NOT A PRISON MAKE'

THE GENERAL ELECTION of 1918 resulted in a great victory for Sinn Féin. Members held meetings in January in preparation for the first session of Dáil Éireann on 21 January 1919. Éamon de Valera being still a prisoner in Lincoln Jail, Cathal Brugha was elected acting president. Collins was appointed minister of home affairs. He did not attend the opening session of the Dáil. Characteristically, he was engaged in important work behind the scenes: the rescue of de Valera from prison.

De Valera had been thinking of making his escape for some time. He noticed that the prison chaplain, for whom he served Mass, often left keys lying around. If an impression could be made of them and sent out to friends in Ireland, a key could be made to open a door in the prison wall that led straight out to fields and the main road. De Valera succeeded in making an impression with the aid of a wax candle. A clever plan was used to send out a copy of the impression without arousing suspicion. As it was now the Christmas season, one of the prisoners, Seán Milroy, made a postcard with two pictures on it headed 'Christmas 1917 and Christmas 1918'. The first picture showed a drunken man trying vainly to insert a latchkey into his hall door, saying 'I can't get in!' In the other picture, the same man was in a prison cell holding an outsize key and complaining: 'I can't get out!' The key was an exact copy of the impression taken by de Valera.

The postcard was smuggled out with an explanatory letter. Unfortunately, only the postcard arrived in Dublin, so that its meaning was lost on the readers.

A second message was then smuggled out in Irish and brought to Ireland to Collins at the house of Mrs Seán McGarry. A key was made and baked in a cake made by Mrs McGarry. However, when it was sent to the prisoners in Lincoln, the key was found to be too small. A second key was made and put in another cake. Alas, it also proved defective. Work began on a third key. Meanwhile, Peadar DeLoughry, another prisoner, had succeeded in removing the lock of a disused cell. He found it was a quadruple lock and that the chaplain's key was not a master key. He requested that the third key be sent to him to finish, together with some locksmith's tools. This was done and great was the joy of the prisoners when the locksmith produced a master key for de Valera.

It was now decided that two other prisoners should join de Valera in the escape. They were Seán Milroy and Seán McGarry.

On 3 February 1919 Michael Collins, Harry Boland and Paddy O'Donoghue of Manchester arrived in Lincoln by taxi from Newark. When darkness fell, Collins and

Boland crossed the fields to the back wall of the prison. Here, they signalled to the prisoners by flashing a lamp. The prisoners answered by lighting matches at their window. All was now ready. The rescuers drew near to the prison door only to find their way barred by an iron gate. Collins inserted a duplicate key into it. To his horror, the key broke in the lock. Meanwhile, the three prisoners opened the door of the prison and stepped out in their turn to the gate. Piaras Béaslaí describes what followed:

> Collins said, in a heart-broken tone, 'I've broken a key in the lock, Dev.' De Valera uttered something and tried to thrust his own key into the lock from the other side. By an extraordinary piece of luck he succeeded in pushing out the broken key with his own, and opening the gate.
>
> They made their way across the fields, passing some off-duty soldiers whom Boland

greeted with 'Cheerio, mates', as they walked to Lincoln. Here, the three escaped captives were put into the taxi with O'Donoghue, while Collins and Boland proceeded to London by train.

O'Donoghue conveyed his charges to Sheffield and thence to Manchester. In three weeks all were back, safe and sound, in Dublin.

Now followed a series of escapes, planned by Collins to 'keep the pot boiling', as he said. The first was Robert Barton's moonlit flight from Mountjoy. A fortnight later, on 29 March, twenty Sinn Féin prisoners, including Piaras Béaslaí, escaped in broad daylight while the prisoners were taking exercise. At a given signal, they rushed to a spot at the prison wall where a rope ladder had been thrown over by Peadar Clancy from outside. They climbed over the wall and down the canal bank, where they made good their escape in trams and on bicycles.

An even more spectacular escape was that of six Irish prisoners from Manchester Jail on 25 October 1919. The leaders were Austin Stack and Piaras Béaslaí, who had been re-captured in May. One of the prisoners, Fionán Lynch – who was released on completing his sentence – brought out information to Paddy O'Donoghue in Manchester. The matter was then laid before Collins in Dublin. He sent for Rory O'Connor to make the arrangements.

The prisoners meanwhile devised a code for use in letters opened by the prison censor. Much useful information was exchanged, including news of 'Angela' (Michael) and 'Maude' (O'Donoghue).

One day, Austin Stack was informed that a visitor had arrived to see him. You can imagine his surprise to find that it was Collins himself, under an assumed name. News was exchanged without difficulty, despite the presence of a warder.

The escape was finally fixed for the evening

of Saturday 11 October 1919. The Irish prisoners had permission to take exercise in a yard behind a spiked wall for half an hour at five o'clock. There was only one warder present in the yard. It was proposed to overpower him and throw a stone over a spikeless portion of the wall as a signal to the rescuers waiting outside with a rope ladder.

A disappointment was in store. On Saturday morning, Paddy O'Donoghue visited one of the prisoners. He gave him a note for Stack which explained that the attempt might have to be postponed. If the prisoners in the yard heard three whistles outside the prison wall at five o'clock, they would know that the escape would not take place. And so it proved. The Dublin members of the rescue team had arrived in Manchester but had been unable to find the meeting place in time.

The days which followed were long for the prisoners. There was another exchange of letters. The day fixed for the second attempt was 25 October, again a Saturday. Three of the prisoners overpowered the warder on duty and locked him up in one of the prison cells, while another signalled to the rescuers. Then the six prisoners gathered at the appointed spot at the spikeless part of the wall and waited. A rope with a weight attached was thrown over, but it did not reach far enough to be caught by them. It was withdrawn and thrown over again and again, without success. Moments of terrible suspense followed before Peadar Clancy's head appeared over the wall to see what was the cause of the delay. Seeing the situation at a glance, he moved along the wall to the rope and lowered it until it was within reach. The rope ladder then followed. Up and over the wall went the six prisoners and slid down on the other side. Except for Béaslaí, who injured his arm, all came down safely. They were then spirited away to various destinations, Stack and Béaslaí arriving at the house of an Irish sympathiser in a suburb of Manchester.

At 5.55 on Saturday evening, a telegram was handed in at Manchester addressed to one of Collins's covering addresses in Rathmines. Sent in a mood of high spirits, it read:

> *Letter received. Will arrive on sixth. Family well.*
>
> *George Windsor.*

The use of his Britannic Majesty's name in the telegram seems to have passed unnoticed.

Collins crossed to England and visited Stack and Béaslaí. With Neill Kerr, he arranged their transport home.

When the stowaways disembarked on the quayside in Dublin, they found that Collins – with his usual thoughtfulness – had sent Joe O'Reilly with a car to bring them to Batt O'Connor's house in Donnybrook.

THE DÁIL LOAN

To RETURN TO Dáil Éireann, Mr de Valera slipped back to Dublin and took part in private sessions of the Dáil in April 1919. He was elected president of Dáil Éireann and nominated the following as his ministers: Arthur Griffith (home affairs), Michael Collins (finance), Cathal Brugha (defence), Count Plunkett (foreign affairs), W. T. Cosgrave (local government), Countess Markievicz (labour), Eoin MacNeill (industries) and Robert Barton (agriculture).

At a public session of the Dáil in Dublin's Mansion House, de Valera referred to the need for funds for the new government. When governments are in need of funds, they often decide to ask the ordinary people for a loan of their money, and they reward them with an annual 'interest' each year until the loan is repaid.

The minister for finance was directed to seek a national loan of £1,000,000. Initially a quarter of this sum would be sought from the public at home, and a like amount from abroad. And so the famous Dáil Loan was born.

'Sinn Féin could never collect more than a few thousand pounds,' said Arthur Griffith to Michael Collins.

'Oh, don't worry, we will get £250,000,' replied the young man with his usual self-confidence. And straightaway, he set to work.

The Ministry of Finance of the newly formed government was accommodated temporarily in the headquarters of Sinn Féin at No. 6 Harcourt Street (now the headquarters of Conradh na Gaeilge). Finance occupied part of the second floor. There, the minister and his small staff prepared for the launching of the Dáil Loan.

The Sinn Féin premises were subject to frequent police raids. On 12 September, when work was in progress, a large raiding party of uniformed police and detectives from G Division of the Dublin Metropolitan Police swooped. One of these men, who knew the minister of finance's appearance, decided to search the top floor, while a colleague, who did not know him, came to investigate the small Finance Department. The 'wanted' man was seated at his desk. He proceeded to rebuke the detective, giving his opinion of Irishmen such as he 'who served their country thus'. It became clear that the minister of finance's identity was unknown to the detective. The detective left the room and met the colleague who had completed a search of the upper floor. They proceeded into a room opposite, while the minister of finance slipped carefully upstairs and luckily escaped arrest.

No. 76 Harcourt Street became the home of the Department of Finance and some other departments of Dáil Éireann. Finance occupied the second floor. In one room, secret hiding places for documents were skilfully inserted in the alcoves by Batt O'Connor, who was a builder. On 11 November 1919 a large force of police, accompanied by military with fixed bayonets, appeared at the entrance. Some men who had called to do business in the various offices were on the premises. They included the commanding officer of the Dublin Brigade, Dick McKee, and Frank Lawless, TD, among others.

The minister of finance was working at his desk on the second floor. Documents were quickly arranged in the hiding places, and the minister, donning hat and coat, went up to the top floor and out through a skylight onto the roof. He worked his way along the house tops and entered the Standard Hotel through the skylight. Unfortunately, it opened onto the well of the stairs. Collins saw that to jump straight down meant certain death. Instead, he hung from the skylight and swung his body over the banisters, clearing the well by inches. He related afterwards to his friends: 'Just as I got through the hotel skylight I saw a khaki helmet appear out of the skylight of No. 76. I flung my bag before me, said a prayer, and jumped.' He then continued down the stairs until he met a friendly member of the staff who, having brushed down his 'guest', escorted him to a hackney car – and so, to safety.

All male members of the staff found in '76' on that occasion were arrested and jailed. ('We are not taking the ladies today,' announced the burly superintendent cheerfully.) The premises were closed and the Finance Department went underground until the Truce. Its offices were situated in many places: Cullenswood House, Bachelor's Walk, Camden Street, Mary Street, Mrs Margaret McGarry's house, 31 Fitzwilliam Street, Harcourt Terrace and often in the homes of sympathisers.

Organising the national loan was a task

well suited to the experience and skills of the minister of finance. It appealed to his essentially constructive and practical mind. He prepared a set of conditions for the loan – called a prospectus – which was inserted as an advertisement into the Irish weekly papers. 'The proceeds of the Loan,' he wrote 'will be used for propagating the Irish case all over the world: for establishing in foreign countries Consular Services to promote Irish Trade and Commerce; for developing and encouraging Irish Sea Fisheries; for developing and encouraging re-afforestation of the country; for developing and encouraging Irish industrial effort ... for establishing National Arbitration Courts.'

All the papers that carried the advertisement were suppressed by the British authorities, who declared the loan illegal. These measures only served to strengthen its support.

Detailed instructions were made out

for the organisers. Collins pointed out the importance of not neglecting to try for support among persons not known to be in the movement. He realised that many businessmen would be unwilling to subscribe openly for fear that their business would suffer at the hands of crown forces. In fact, later on, when lists of subscribers' names were captured by the enemy during a raid, the authorities were most disagreeably surprised to find among them the names of many supposedly 'loyal' citizens!

When the Loan closed, Collins had the satisfaction of reporting that the subscriptions in Ireland had reached £379,000 – £129,000 more than he had anticipated. He was also much gratified by the fact that his own county of Cork had performed particularly well.

The main fund in notes was deposited in the bank. The gold – £25,000 – was given to Batt O'Connor, who buried it under the concrete floor of his house in Donnybrook. Here it remained, in spite of many raids, until it was handed over to the auditor general of Dáil Éireann in 1922.

Éamon de Valera announced his intention of going to America to enlist help for the Irish cause. The idea had come to him in Lincoln Jail, and he now felt that as president of Dáil Éireann and a citizen of the United States of America, he would be in a position to work there effectively for recognition of Ireland's claims, and to publicise the Dáil Loan among the Irish-American communities.

Collins made the arrangements. De Valera, disguised as a sailor, was smuggled to New York aboard the *Celtic*. He was to be absent from Ireland until December 1920. The battles waged on both sides of the Atlantic during the intervening period – though very different – were grim and unremitting: de Valera in the midst of the conflicts of Irish-American politics, and Collins in the horrors of the Black and Tan war. In spite of the difficulties, they remained in close touch with each other. In his disagreements with Irish-American politicians, de Valera was loyally supported by his colleagues at home, led by Collins. Not only that, Collins also made it his business to pay regular visits to Mrs de Valera and her children at Greystones, and saw to it that letters and news of them reached the Irish president in America. When Mrs de Valera paid a visit to her husband in America, it was Collins's 'services' that provided her with the necessary documents and arranged for her passage.

IRELAND'S FIRST FINANCE MINISTER

MICHAEL COLLINS WAS now in his thirtieth year. Oliver St John Gogarty recalls 'the un-lined face and the beautiful, womanly hands', and the 'skin … like undiscoloured ivory'.

Simone Tery, a French journalist, wrote: 'At first sight the minister of finance looks like a *bon vivant*. Thirty years old, thick dark hair, open forehead, full face … When he is serious … one notices that his keen eyes are piercing; he has a square jaw, tight lips, an energetic chin …' When he laughed, she thought that the sight of such good humour should be enough to invigorate the whole of Ireland!

But not all his acquaintances thought so highly of him. It was to be expected that so energetic, active and resourceful a person should irritate more staid persons, especially those for whom good intentions were a substitute for work well done. His bold and determined language, together with his intolerance of slackness and inefficiency, made him enemies.

Some thought he interfered too much in the work of other departments. The 'interference', however, was always constructive; it took the form of assistance and guidance necessary to make the different departments work smoothly together. Nowadays, we would say that his role was that of a co-ordinator.

To the Volunteer companies throughout the country, Collins was the man who got things done, the man to see in Dublin. Dan Breen testified to this fact when he wrote that Collins 'was the member of GHQ [General Headquarters] who stood by us consistently'.

It was the British government itself which gave him public recognition as the chief architect of resistance to it, when a price of £10,000 was put on his head. The personal publicity which he had never sought was now thrust upon him. That some of his colleagues were human enough to resent all this was to be expected. Though younger than many of them, he held several key posts in Dáil Éireann and in the Volunteer Executive. His position in the IRB was viewed with suspicion by those who believed that the Irish Volunteers, now the army of Dáil Éireann, rendered the IRB unnecessary. Some of his critics feared that his position in the IRB might add to his personal power, forgetting that energy and a quick brain have always helped their possessor.

As he was always in a hurry, Collins often appeared abrupt to those who did not know him well. He was not tactful when criticising laziness and inefficiency. Dismissing the work of one department of the Dáil, he told the minister responsible: 'Everyone knows that your department is a bloody joke.' The remark was never forgotten.

To his own staff, he was the key man in the Anglo-Irish war. In serving him, they were serving Ireland. They worked hard, but they saw how much harder he worked. And in his busy and hard-pressed existence, he never omitted to show his appreciation of their efforts. His complete dedication commanded their loyalty and respect.

In his few hours of leisure, he was the sunniest and merriest of companions, but there was nothing of the casual, happy-go-lucky Irishman about him. Although he frequently met detectives and collaborators in public houses, he drank as little as possible. The dangerous life he led was such that he could not allow his faculties to be impaired by indulgence in the national weakness. He also gave up smoking early in the campaign. 'I'll be a slave to nothing,' he said.

Michael Collins did not regard himself as a politician. And this would appear to be a correct assumption. He did not possess that 'toughness' in the realm of feeling which is a characteristic of the more successful political figures, enabling them to survive disasters and the loss of friends and still persevere. He was a sensitive man whose feelings were deep. Those in misfortune experienced his kindness and consideration. It was this kindness, hidden under an often stern exterior, that caused Barney Mellows to call him the Dark Angel. Quite without malice and envy himself, he perhaps underrated these defects in others. Before his death he was to experience some of their fruits.

ON HIS KEEPING

BETWEEN MOREHAMPTON ROAD and Herbert Park in Dublin lies a quiet residential area. Most of the houses were built at the turn of the century for prosperous, mostly 'loyal' dwellers, as indicated by the names of the roads: Argyle Road, Victoria Avenue.

Brendan Road was built by a devoted follower of Collins who had prospered in the building trade in America: Batt O'Connor. A Kerryman and a 1916 man, O'Connor's loyalties were reflected in the name chosen for the new road where he lived with his family. A skilled carpenter, he constructed secret rooms and cupboards in various houses used by Michael and his staff. Collins himself was a frequent visitor to Brendan Road and had some narrow escapes there.

O'Connor was often uneasy because his guest took so few precautions:

I was often struck by the bold way he would open the hall door, marching out with his head up, and with firm footsteps, the sound of which could be heard through the whole street. Often I was on the point of exclaiming, 'Damn it, man, don't make so much noise' … I would hear his loud footsteps echoing down the whole length of Brendan Road.

This bold, self-confident manner of his often struck me in contrast with the ways of other men. They would only leave my hall door with the greatest of care, peering round it to see who might be outside, and drawing down their caps well over their eyes before venturing forth. He had a great contempt for these manoeuvres and said such men were asking for trouble.

As the Dublin detective force became less and less effective, the British decided to send down from Belfast a certain Mr Redmond, who was a most efficient man. He was appointed second-assistant commissioner of the Dublin Metropolitan Police, with the special duty of reorganising the detective force. He made no secret of the fact that he was determined to 'get his man'.

At the same time, another British agent arrived in Dublin. Under the name of Jameson, this man had passed himself off as a revolutionary in British socialist circles. In reality, he was an agent of Scotland Yard. Armed with a letter of introduction from a Sinn Féin representative in London, he succeeded in meeting Collins. He was later referred to Tom Cullen and Liam Tobin. Fortunately, Cullen distrusted Jameson from the first – a circumstance that probably saved Collins's life.

It was not long before Jameson was able to report to Redmond that he had an appointment to meet Collins at Batt O'Connor's house at lunchtime on the following day. Mr Redmond made his arrangements accordingly. A detective was posted at the top of Brendan

Road to watch O'Connor's house. A lorry full of detectives was sent from the Castle to intercept Collins.

Meanwhile, Jameson – who had finished his business with Collins – left the house with Liam Tobin. The detective watching the house assumed that one of them was Collins, and rushed back along the Morehampton Road to meet the oncoming lorry. When the driver stopped, he called to him, 'Too late – there's no point in going on. The bird has flown. Better come back again tomorrow at the same time.'

A friendly detective reported to Collins that Redmond, who was in the lorry, had scolded them all for their failure in tracking down the quarry, 'considering that a man just over from England had been able to see him'. Obviously, this was Jameson. To make sure of his guilt, a trap was set for him next day. Collins, cycling along Morehampton Road, saw a detective posted near Brendan Road.

Collins turned into Brendan Road, and noted that the detective jumped on a passing tram to phone the Castle from nearby Donnybrook Barracks. His quarry meanwhile cycled down and out at the end of Brendan Road without calling at the O'Connor house. The raiding party led by Redmond duly arrived and burst into the O'Connor home. They found only Mrs O'Connor and the children. The house was searched from top to bottom with no result. Not satisfied with this, Redmond returned during the night and watched and listened outside the windows in the vain hope of hearing something that would tell him where the wanted man was.

Three days later Redmond was shot dead near the Standard Hotel in Harcourt Street. Jameson crossed to England to report to his employers. On his return, he made another attempt to contact Collins. He arranged to meet one of the intelligence staff on a lonely road on the outskirts of Dublin. When he reached the meeting place, he was captured and executed, as is the fate of spies in wartime. His death caused a sensation in England when the socialists discovered that he was, in reality, an agent of the British government.

Collins had another narrow escape at his personal office in Mespil Road. The house was occupied by a journalist, Miss Hoey, and her mother. Miss Hoey's name had been found on a list of members of Cumann na mBan in the possession of the enemy – hence the raid. It took place on 1 April 1921, after curfew. As the house had also been provided with a secret compartment into which files and documents were deposited each evening, nothing of importance was discovered. But some miscellaneous papers and evidence of an office being in use aroused suspicion. The raiding party took possession of the office, and having questioned Miss Hoey – who professed ignorance of the nature of the work carried on by her tenant, 'Mr O'Brien' – they occupied the apartment. Supported by armed intelligence officers from the Castle, they settled down to await the arrival of 'Mr O'Brien' and his staff next morning.

Miss Hoey now found herself in a difficult position. How could she save Collins from walking into the trap?

When she and her mother retired to their bedroom, they decided that the mother, a delicate lady, would pretend to be taken ill so that a doctor would have to be called. The old lady bravely played her part, and Miss Hoey told the guard at the bedroom door that a doctor must be sent for immediately. They told her that she must go herself, but that a guard would go with her.

Accompanied by soldiers in plain clothes, Miss Hoey set off for the house of Dr Alice Barry, a trusted friend of Michael Collins. Fortunately, the doctor understood the situation at once. Having attended the patient, she returned home and early next morning contacted Mr McCluskey, caretaker of the Land Bank in Leeson Street. He alerted the people known to him, including the staff member who would have been first into the lion's den that morning. Those who knew Collins were recruited to intercept him. All approaches to Mespil Road were kept under observation. Collins was halted cycling through town, and Joe O'Reilly came to announce the good news to all the 'friends'.

THE BLACK AND TANS ARE HERE!

IRELAND WAS NOW openly at war with the forces of British rule. Attacks were carried out on barracks in different parts of the country, and successful raids were made for arms. This, together with the ostracising of members of the RIC, had a disastrous effect on recruitment. Many barracks in country districts closed down altogether for lack of policemen.

The administration of the country was now in the hands of Dáil Éireann. Even the law courts had given way to the Sinn Féin courts. So impartial and just were the decisions of these courts that they were used by nationalists and unionists alike. British intelligence had been successfully penetrated. At this train of mounting disaster, the British government looked first with disbelief and then with a mounting sense of outrage. It was undoubtedly the success of the Dáil Loan which showed them quite clearly that – for the first time since the Battle of Benburb – they were facing a united, disciplined and confident enemy. For the British, the situation was serious. Strong measures were needed. So the Black and Tans came into being.

Advertisements for recruits for 'a rough and dangerous task' appeared in the British newspapers. The men who joined up – if not all inmates of British jails, as was believed in Ireland – were of a very different kind to the military. Many had fought in the Great War and were now demobilised and unemployed. It was clear from the beginning that army discipline was not for them. Their job, according to their weekly paper, was 'making Ireland once again safe for the law-abiding, and an appropriate hell for those whose trade is agitation and whose method is murder'. Their own actions in Ireland were reminiscent of English repression in 1798.

As there were no uniforms for them when they arrived, they dressed in a combination of black RIC and khaki uniforms, earning themselves the name 'Black and Tans'. This sinister force was later joined by another body of men known as Auxiliaries. Many of these were ex-officers of the British Army, and received higher pay than the Black and Tans.

The war was intensified. In their search for arms, documents and wanted men, the Black and Tans raided houses and offices. People were held up in the street and searched. Lorries full of Black and Tans, with their rifles pointed towards onlookers, terrorised town and country alike. Attacks on Black and Tans often resulted in people being taken from their beds and shot as a reprisal. Most of the victims had no connection with the Volunteers. Curfew was imposed, requiring all the inhabitants to be indoors from midnight until 5 a.m.

The efforts of the Volunteers were not lessened by these measures. The Dublin Castle mails were intercepted by Volunteers, for example. The official correspondence was opened, yielding much useful information. Another successful action that dealt the British administration a heavy blow was the burning of income-tax offices in different parts of the country by groups of Volunteers. The operation was a complete success, rendering payment of income tax impossible. Even the British recognised that it was a well-organised and concerted coup.

On the night of 20 March 1920, Tomás MacCurtain, lord mayor of Cork, was murdered in the presence of his wife by members of the RIC.

Terence MacSwiney, a close friend of the murdered man, succeeded him as lord mayor of Cork. On the day he became mayor, MacSwiney made what has been described as 'one of the greatest speeches in Irish history':

… I come here more as a soldier stepping into the breach than as an administrator to fill the first post in the Municipality … We see in the manner in which our late Lord Mayor was murdered an attempt to terrify us all. Our first duty is to answer that threat in the only fitting manner, by showing ourselves unterrified – cool and inflexible for the fulfilment of our chief purpose – the establishment of the independence and integrity of our country … I was more closely associated than any other here with our late murdered friend and colleague, both before and since the events of the Easter Week, in prison and out of it, in a common work of love for Ireland, down to the hour of his death. For that reason I take his place. It is, I think, though I say it, the only fitting answer to those who struck him down.

On 12 August MacSwiney was himself arrested and sentenced to two years' imprisonment. He went on hunger strike and was transferred to Brixton prison in London, where, after seventy-three days, he died.

Arthur Griffith spoke at his funeral, concluding with the memorable words:

Mourn for him but let your mourning be that for a martyr who triumphs. Ireland has lost a noble son, as France lost a noble daughter when Saint Joan of Arc perished in the English bonfire. The sequel will be the same. Saint Joan of Arc has, in him, welcomed a comrade to heaven.

THE FIRST BLOODY SUNDAY

THE BLACK AND Tans continued to terrorise the people all over the country. They burned, destroyed and murdered at will. Dáil Éireann had neither the men nor the equipment to match the forces of the crown, but realised that something would have to be done about them and those who helped them.

A cabinet meeting of the Dáil discussed a proposal to assassinate members of the British cabinet as a reprisal. This was rejected because it would lose Ireland the support of many good and just Englishmen, and because cabinet ministers could be replaced overnight. A strict rule was made: only proven spies and informers should be executed. Their knowledge would die with them and their fate would stop others from following in their footsteps. All executions were to be carried out under the authority of Dáil Éireann and sanctioned by General Headquarters. That the laws of war were uniformly observed on the Irish side was due to the discipline and idealism of the Volunteers.

Towards the end of 1920, the British decided that it was time to put an end once and for all to the activities of Michael Collins and his associates. 'They think when they get me everything will be over,' said Collins laughingly to Béaslaí. Characteristically, he added: 'They'll get the hell of a drop.' He was now to get a taste of a really serious attempt to destroy him and his organisation.

A group of British officers with training in intelligence work arrived in Dublin. Their task was to track down Collins and his associates. Prior warning of their intentions had been received through the usual channels. The information was duly laid before a meeting of General Headquarters. The decision was then taken to order the execution of twenty members of the gang, whose guilt was not in doubt.

The day fixed was Sunday 21 November 1920, known in the annals of Irish history as 'Bloody Sunday'.

On Saturday night, Collins, Dick McKee, Peadar Clancy, Piaras Béaslaí and some others were holding a meeting in the smoke-room of Vaughan's Hotel in Parnell Square. When the meeting broke up, Dick McKee left first. Collins was the last to leave. Piaras Béaslaí and another man, Seán O'Connell, stayed behind talking to Conor Clune – a young Volunteer from Clare – in a small room under the stairs. Clune had no know-ledge of what was planned.

The young lad who was keeping watch on the street now came running in to announce, 'It's the Tans!'

Collins himself had barely had time to reach a house a few doors down the square, where he was able to watch the raid from an upper window.

Knowing that the party in the smoke-room had gotten away safely, Béaslaí and Seán O'Connell sensibly stayed where they were. The Auxiliaries burst in and rushed up to the smoke-room, showing the accuracy of their information. In the confusion that followed, Béaslaí and O'Connell managed to slip out the back door to the garden. A military lorry, with a searchlight shining on the rear of the hotel, was stationed in the lane at the back. Béaslaí had to stay crouched under a wall until the Auxiliaries had departed. Seán O'Connell managed to escape by telling the Auxiliary on guard that he had come out of one of the small houses on the lane to go home to Dorset Street. Poor Conor Clune did not fare so well. He was arrested and taken away in a lorry to Dublin Castle. His innocence was to afford him no protection.

Worse was to come. Later that night, Dick McKee and Peadar Clancy were arrested.

On Sunday morning, members of the Dublin Brigade and the special 'Squad' assigned for duty made their way to various lodging houses around the city. They shot dead fourteen men and wounded five others. Of two of their targets lodging in Mount Street, one was shot and the other escaped by locking himself into his room and barricading the door. The sound of firing drew the Auxiliaries to the scene in time to exchange shots with the attacking party, one of whom was wounded and captured.

As the news had not reached the public, life in Dublin went on as usual. A GAA match between Dublin and Tipperary was to be held that afternoon in Croke Park. It was in full progress when lorries full of British forces suddenly appeared on the scene. Training their guns on both players and spectators, they opened fire, killing fourteen people and injuring sixty, not to mention those trampled underfoot by the panic-stricken crowds.

On Monday morning, Dick McKee, Peadar Clancy and Conor Clune were taken out and shot in Dublin Castle. The first two had been cruelly tortured, presumably to get them to betray their comrades. The death of the three young men was a cause of sorrow and shock to Collins. The loss of McKee and Clancy was also a great blow to the cause. The handsome Dick McKee had been one of Michael's closest friends.

The British authorities issued a false statement claiming that the three men had been shot 'while attempting to escape'. Collins arranged for a medical examination to be carried out on the bodies during the night, while they lay in the Pro-Cathedral. The examination, at which he was present, showed the torments inflicted on McKee and Clancy, and completely disproved the falsehoods of Dublin Castle.

Collins was among the congregation present at the Requiem Mass on the following day. No enemy recognised him as he helped to carry out the coffins of his friends.

The deaths of the intelligence officers on Bloody Sunday caused fear and confusion in the British cabinet. Precautions for protecting the ministers were reinforced. 'All my household are armed,' declared Sir Hamar Greenwood at a cabinet conference on 25 November, 'my valet, my butler and my cook. So if you have any complaints about the soup, you know what to expect.'

TOWARDS A TRUCE

THE BRITISH REIGN of terror continued unabated. The office of *The Freemen's Journal* was burnt by crown forces on 29 November 1920. The burning was in reprisal for the coverage given by the paper to the misdeeds of the British forces. The culminating point was reached with the burning of Cork city by troops on 11 December. Although Sir Hamar Greenwood was shameless enough to state that the city had been burned down by its inhabitants, the truth could not be concealed.

The Volunteers achieved some notable victories about this time. One of the most famous was the Kilmichael ambush in which a party of Auxiliaries was attacked and only one survived. The 'Flying Columns' were especially active in the south of Ireland and in Longford, under the able leadership of Tom Barry, Liam Lynch and Seán MacEoin.

In the country, it could be said that the Irish Republican Army (IRA) had the upper hand; in the cities, the Auxiliaries still held sway.

After Bloody Sunday, Arthur Griffith, the acting president of Dáil Éireann while de Valera was in America, was arrested and lodged in Mountjoy. His first action was to appoint Michael Collins as acting president in his place.

Griffith had been working for Ireland when most of his colleagues were children. An outstanding journalist and a man of firm and upright character, his writings provided the basis of the philosophy of the Sinn Féin movement. At a time when a physical-force movement was only a dream, he had fought the British authorities single-handed – with his pen. He had been linked with many colourful figures of pre-1914 Dublin: Madame Markievicz, Maud Gonne and W. B. Yeats. That the message of his writings had fallen on fruitful soil was plain for all to see in the young men who flocked to join the Volunteers. Now in his middle years, Griffith worked closely with younger men, who put what was essentially his programme into action. Although not himself a combatant, Griffith fully supported the armed action of the Volunteers. In naming Collins as his deputy, he showed his confidence in him.

Yet another responsibility was now laid on Collins's shoulders. At this time, the British prime minister, a Welshman named David Lloyd George, was secretly trying to sound out the Irish on the possibility of holding peace talks. This made matters more complicated for Collins because he saw what was a military situation beginning to develop into a political one. One of Lloyd George's emissaries was Archbishop Clune of Perth, Australia, who was a relative of the murdered Conor Clune. Doubtless, the Welshman thought that a prominent ecclesiastic might meet with a favourable reception in Ireland.

The archbishop arrived in Ireland in December and met Arthur Griffith in Mountjoy and Collins elsewhere. He was told that the Irish were willing to negotiate provided that all acts of violence on both sides should cease and that Dáil Éireann should be free to meet without interference from the authorities.

Dr Clune returned to London to be told by Lloyd George that there could be no question of a truce unless the Irish first surrendered their arms, a condition not mentioned before.

Griffith told the archbishop that the British wanted surrender, not a truce, and that there would be no surrender. The prospects for peace talks seemed slight.

Lloyd George, however, had made progress on another front. On 23 December 1920 the Government of Ireland Act was passed by his government, partitioning Ireland and setting up two governments – one in Dublin and one in Belfast for the unionists who would not consider being ruled from Dublin. The full implications of the act were probably not grasped on the Irish side (although Collins called it a 'plunderous and impossible Act').

Éamon de Valera's return from America was a relief to all. That evening, Collins, in a fit of optimism, invited some of his friends to dine with him in the Gresham Hotel. As the Gresham was frequented by British spies, Michael's invitation looked more like an act of defiance than anything else. His friends, who did not like to see him go alone into the wolf's den, accepted. Down they went to O'Connell Street – Michael, Gearóid O'Sullivan, Rory O'Connor, Tom Cullen and Liam Tobin.

When they arrived, they were informed that there was no private room available and that they would have to take their seats in the public dining-room. They did so, and had barely finished their meal when they were informed by a waiter that a party of Auxiliaries had arrived and was inquiring about the men who had requested a private room. A minute later, the Auxiliaries burst into the dining-room and surrounded them.

'Stand up!' said the officer to Collins.

He rose immediately, pretending to be indignant.

'What is your name?' said the officer.

'John Grace,' replied Michael Collins.

'What is your job?' said the officer. 'Where do you work?'

'I am an accountant,' said Collins quickly. 'My office is in Dame Street.'

The officer insisted on searching him. He found only an Ordnance Survey map on which Collins had written what looked like '6 refills' to remind himself of something.

'6 rifles!' exclaimed the officer.

'Not rifles – refills,' said Collins. 'What would I want with rifles? I use notebooks for which I often need refills. Look!' And with a smile, he produced his notebook. But the officer continued to look at him with suspicion. Suddenly, he thrust his hand into his pocket and pulled out an old photograph of Collins. He even ran his fingers through his hair the better to compare his face with the photograph. Michael continued to smile, though inwardly preparing to snatch the officer's revolver and make a dash for safety.

After what seemed a very long time, the officer released him and stepped back, motioning to his men to follow him out. This was the narrowest escape Michael Collins ever had.

RESCUE

A MEETING OF Dáil Éireann was now called, at which de Valera put forward a suggestion that the war effort should be relaxed so as to create an atmosphere that would help the peace negotiations. There was no support for this. Nearly all the members present agreed with Collins that such a course would only give the enemy reason to believe that the Volunteers were weakening. Any settlement would have to be negotiated from a position of strength.

So the war was intensified. Curfew now began at 9 p.m. Ambushes, raids, hold-ups and reprisals continued worse than ever. In Dublin the people became accustomed to bombs and combat in the city streets by day. Military lorries roared through towns, carrying citizens chained on them as hostages.

Collins usually met his friends in the

detective force at a house in Clontarf. One evening, having finished their business, they all left the house together and he offered them a lift into town in his car – or rather, Joe Hyland's car, which was kept for his use. On the way, they were halted by soldiers who had just been ambushed at Newcomen Bridge. The officer asked for their passes and, on 'learning' they were policemen, told them all about the ambush.

Collins spoke up wrathfully: 'These ambushes are disgraceful!'

'Yes, and if you saw how they came on us,' began the officer, launching into a detailed description of the action.

But Collins interrupted him: 'Send us a report at the Castle immediately. We'll have it in the morning.' And he got back into the car and they drove safely away.

The authorities now decided to carry out a reprisal against Collins himself. If they could not capture him, his family would suffer. The

Collins family home at Woodfield was occupied by Michael's eldest brother, John, whose wife had died a short time before, leaving eight children. One day, when the master of the house was absent in Cork, members of the Essex Regiment arrived at Woodfield with orders to burn the house and its contents. The occupants were ordered to leave without bringing anything with them except clothing for the baby. Later that day John was intercepted on his way home on the train and sent to be interned on Spike Island.

Collins was greatly distressed at the destruction of his family home, to which he had always been greatly attached. In the midst of a life filled with responsibility, difficulties and dangers, he had always been able to think of Woodfield as a haven of peace and security. Now it was gone, leaving him only memories.

There were other matters needing his attention, however. The arrest of Seán MacEoin in Mullingar had deprived the IRA of one of its best officers. Collins was determined to try to rescue him from Mountjoy Jail, where he awaited a court martial.

A British armoured car was ambushed and captured by five Volunteers, none of whom had ever driven such a vehicle before. Undaunted, they picked up Emmet Dalton, the assistant director of training, who had served in the British Army during the Great War. He was wearing his old army uniform. On arrival at the prison, they were immediately admitted. Dalton and another Volunteer, armed with a forged order directing the transfer of the prisoner, made their way into the governor's office, where they captured not only the governor, but six others as well.

To prevent the main gate from being closed before the armoured car got out again, two more Volunteers appeared with a parcel and tried to engage the gate-keeper in conversation about visiting the prison. However, he would answer no questions, and proceeded to close the gate in full view of the sentry, who fired on them. He in turn was fired on by one of the Volunteers in the car. The sound of the firing alerted the Volunteers inside the building to the fact that their intention had been discovered. There was nothing for it but to beat a hasty retreat to the armoured car and get out as quickly as possible. This they did, driving the armoured car out of Mountjoy, not stopping until they got to Clontarf. Fortunately, they had suffered no casualties, except for one man who was slightly wounded in the wrist.

Collins was bitterly disappointed. Up to the last moment before the court martial, he was still thinking up plans for MacEoin's rescue. At the court martial, MacEoin defended his actions with dignity and courage. Three Auxiliaries captured by him at Ballinalee testified to his gallantry and chivalrous behaviour towards them and his care for the wounded.

It was all of no avail. MacEoin was sentenced to death.

THE CUSTOM HOUSE ON FIRE

COLLINS NOW LAUNCHED what was perhaps the biggest operation of the Anglo-Irish war: the burning of the Custom House. Collected there were all the records of local government, customs, Inland Revenue and so on. The Volunteers who took part in the attack numbered 120, the largest number engaged on any operation since the Easter Rising.

At noon on 25 May 1920 a lorry loaded with petrol cans drew up outside the Custom House. A large party of Volunteers rushed into it and collected all the occupants together, while others sprinkled petrol in the offices and corridors. When all was ready, the people were ordered to leave and the building was set on fire.

A lorry load of Auxiliaries happened to pass near a detachment of Volunteers sent to guard the approaches to the Custom

House. Bombs were thrown at the lorry and the alarm brought armoured cars quickly to the scene. The building was now surrounded. Some of the IRA fought their way out; some managed to dump their weapons and mingled with the crowd, but many were captured by the Auxiliaries. The Irish losses were heavy: six killed, twelve wounded and seventy captured. Nevertheless, the burning of the Custom House and its records dealt the English administration in Ireland its death blow and showed the British government that its campaign of 'frightfulness' had failed to break the will of Ireland's freedom fighters.

In June 1921 the king of England travelled to Belfast to open the new parliament. He was said to be a humane man. He had been concerned at the state of affairs in Ireland and had urged Lloyd George to intensify his efforts for peace. The king's speech, which had been prepared in consultation with

Lloyd George, took the form of an appeal to all Irishmen to make peace for the common good of their country. His sentiments, though admirable, took little account of the fact that the quarrel was not between Irishmen, north and south, but between Ireland and England. Lloyd George, who had been sending out feelers for peace talks for some time, now set to work again, this time with better results. A truce was finally agreed upon between the British Army and the IRA, to come into effect on 11 July 1921.

Writing at this time to a friend, Collins commented, 'Now we are going to be really tested. The days ahead are going to be truly trying ones and we can only face them with set faces and hearts full of hope and confidence. It would be very dreadful if we did anything wrong.'

THE TRUCE

To the Volunteers, the Truce brought a much-needed rest, as well as a chance to enlist and train new men. The break in the fighting was welcome: the IRA was hard-pressed by the enemy. Arms and ammunition were scarce. Although they had bravely held the vastly superior forces of the enemy at bay, they had not beaten them. Officers from the southern brigades had come to Dublin to report to General Headquarters that they could not carry on much longer because of lack of ammunition and harassment by the enemy.

The successes on the Irish side were not just military. The destruction of the English administrative system was as great a victory as any military victory could have been.

The end of all military action should be to reach a settlement acceptable to both sides.

Without her fighting force, Ireland's representatives would never have reached the conference table.

Public opinion abroad did not favour the British campaign of repression. Conscious of the world's disapproval and the united determination of the Irish people, the British government saw the need for a settlement of the 'Irish Question'.

Accordingly, invitations were sent to President de Valera to send delegates to a conference 'with a view to ascertaining how the association of Ireland with the community of nations known as the British Empire may best be reconciled with Irish national aspirations'.

It was clear that the British cabinet would not recognise Ireland as a sovereign state. In spite of this, acceptance of the invitation was approved by the Dáil and cabinet.

Some writers hold that accepting an invitation so worded reduced the chances of recognition for a free Irish republic. Many viewed the Truce with misgiving.

Some of the fighting men relaxed. 'Fairweather recruits' enlisted. Few stopped to consider the possibility that the war might begin again. If it did, the prevailing optimism would be the worst preparation for it.

One good thing came of the Truce: it saved the life of Seán MacEoin. When it seemed certain that the British wanted to negotiate, the president and the minister of finance made it clear – each in his own way – that there would be no negotiations unless MacEoin was released. The British complied and MacEoin was freed.

After his release, the valiant 'Blacksmith of Ballinalee' arrived at the Mansion House to attend a meeting of Dáil Éireann. Collins also arrived. Both now found themselves the idols of the crowd that thronged to the public session. The public saw in MacEoin the bravery and chivalry of the warrior, and in Collins the will and moving spirit of the resistance.

Simone Tery, the French journalist, was an eyewitness to MacEoin's reception. This is how she described it:

Is this really he? He is only a lad, this commander. Is he even twenty years old? His eyes shine with joy, his broad smile is that of a child. He shakes hands all round. Introductions are made, he says nothing, he twists his hat round in his fingers and looks both shy and radiant. MacEoin is put sitting down in an armchair and all sit down around him. In a corner, taut and silent stands Griffith, the first, the great worker of the Sinn Féin movement. And here is the celebrated and elusive Michael Collins … he laughs to himself and now and again he laughs aloud and throws back his hair; he is the picture of jubilation … But no one speaks … all devour with their eyes the blushing child who has just escaped death. Mick Collins risks an amusing story – something about a shoe thrown out of the window and the police. No one understands it very well, but it is a good opportunity for giving rein to joy. People rub their hands and exult. Then they are silent again, still looking at the commander. They are not able to make speeches. But nothing could be more eloquent than the silent emotion of these leaders, their heads bent over the smiling and embarrassed face of the 'murderer'.

The minister of finance, however, had no time for the people's worship of himself. Not many journalists got the opportunity of an interview with him. Simone Tery, who was one of the exceptions, described her meeting with him during the Truce.

'You know,' he began, 'I give no interviews.'

'No, of course not, this is not an interview – just a simple conversation, if you prefer.'

'Very well,' he said, reassured. (Strange, she thought, how they are all afraid of the word interview). There was a pause.

'Please tell me some of your adventures,' she said.

Collins began to laugh. 'It is not for me to tell you about them.'

'Oh, yes,' she insisted. 'At least I shall know that they actually occurred.'

He hesitated and thought for a moment. Now, she thought, he is going to speak, and she prompted him. 'The story of the Sister of Charity, is that true? How did you manage to pass yourself off as a woman?' (The minister of finance was strong and broad-shouldered.)

He laughed again and tried to sidetrack her.

'I can't tell you anything … Anyway, I did nothing extraordinary. There were others besides me. Did you know that Bob Barton escaped from Mountjoy?'

'Yes, I know, but we are talking about *you*

today … And the story about your leap into space. It must have been a terrible sensation.'

'Oh, I had no time to think. I had to jump, so I jumped.'

'How did it happen?'

'I haven't yet reached the age for dictating my memoirs!'

Simone Tery lectured him at some length on what would now be called the art of public relations. He needed to make himself better known to the public, she said. So he should talk a little more. He seemed convinced and thought again.

'Well?' she asked, hopefully.

'No, it's impossible, I can't, I just can't do it!' he burst out.

And there she had to leave the matter. His silence and embarrassment impressed her more than any eloquence he could have mustered on his own achievements. She wrote: 'I could not get a single word out of you, yet you gave me the best interview.'

THE TREATY

WE NOW COME to the Treaty and what one historian calls 'the intense personal tragedy of Michael Collins'.

The Treaty itself is too complicated an issue to describe fully in a short book of this kind. When you are older, you will be able to read about it in more detail, and so make up your own mind as to its merits or otherwise.

Bearing in mind the truth of the old saying that 'it is easy to be wise after the event', I have tried to summarise for you a matter which to many people who took sides in the civil war seemed clear-cut and simple, but which in reality was neither.

You may find this part dull reading, but unless you read it through, you will not understand how Irishmen, who had fought side by side for so long, were split into two opposing camps: for and against the Treaty.

This led to a civil war which is known in Irish as *Cogadh na gCarad*.

The time came to select suitable persons to represent the Irish at the peace negotiations in London. It was proposed by William Cosgrave that the president himself should head the delegation. There was little support for the suggestion. De Valera himself considered that, as president, his place was at home. He foresaw that a settlement would involve some compromises unacceptable to some members in his cabinet. By not taking part himself in the talks, he felt that he would be in a better position to influence his colleagues.

As de Valera did not propose to accompany the delegation, Arthur Griffith was chosen as chairman. He was after all vice-president of Dáil Éireann. Cathal Brugha and Austin Stack were asked by the president to go. Understandably, they refused, and he did not insist.

The other members of the delegation chosen were Michael Collins, Robert Barton (minister of economic affairs) and two legal experts: Eamonn Duggan, who had worked with Collins, and George Gavan Duffy, Dáil envoy in Paris and Rome. The secretary was Erskine Childers, assisted by John Chartres, Fionán Lynch and Diarmuid O'Hegarty.

The cabinet now knew that the British would not recognise the Republic. To solve the difficulty and to guide the delegates, President de Valera drew up a draft treaty based on his idea of the future link between Ireland and England. The advantage of this draft was that Ireland would not become a dominion within the British Empire. Instead, Ireland would become what was called an 'external associate', without allegiance to the English crown. And so, the Republic might be preserved in structure if not in name. The word 'Republic' was not actually mentioned, however, and all the president's personal influence was needed to gain acceptance for the document from the strong republicans in his cabinet.

The delegates were instructed not to sign any agreement without first showing it to the cabinet in Dublin. This instruction did not agree with the powers given to them to 'negotiate and conclude … a treaty or treaties of settlement, association and accommodation between Ireland and the community of nations known as the British Commonwealth'.

The British government never seems to have accepted the negotiators as representatives of the Irish Republic. The credentials when offered were simply waved aside by Lloyd George. He knew that to accept or reject them would offend one side or the other and hinder the opening of negotiations.

The British government would have nothing to do with external association. They had accorded dominion status to the South Africans who rose up against them. British public opinion would not tolerate any 'extras' for the Irish, who had caused them so much trouble. Lloyd George knew that to give to Ireland more than the British parliament and public opinion would allow would mean the fall of his government. To him, the Treaty issue was a problem to be solved. To his opponents, it was a matter of life and death.

Lloyd George was no bully, but a politician of great guile and ingenuity. His good humour and charming manner concealed an acute brain that made him a formidable opponent. A native speaker of Welsh, through which he often transacted business, he could be said to be more advanced in the matter of his national language than his opponents. In his younger days, he had tried without success to start a Welsh nationalist party. In all, he was in no way typical of English politicians. As a Celt, he was supposed to be less hostile to the Irish than other members of his cabinet. His record of success in international conferences was phenomenal. Not for nothing is he remembered as the 'Welsh Wizard'.

The difference between the external association document and the proposed Treaty was not great enough to risk war in the eyes of Griffith and Collins. They knew what war was; Collins especially had borne the brunt of it for four years. He had an intimate knowledge of the military situation and the weariness of the people. In the event of a resumption of the war, he could not deceive himself into thinking that the IRA could long stand out against fresh, well-equipped troops.

Neither Griffith nor Collins felt that they could commit themselves to war without the approval of the Dáil and the Irish people.

There remained another difficulty: Ulster. The northern unionists, who were slow to accept a parliament of their own, now declared that they would not come in under an all-Ireland parliament. The Irish delegation insisted that the unity of the country must be preserved at all costs. They were prepared to break the negotiations if this matter was not resolved to their liking.

Lloyd George, who had declared his intention to resign if he failed to achieve Irish unity, did not succeed in forcing the northern prime minister to accept this principle. However, he did not resign. Instead, he sought and found a way out of his difficulty. He succeeded in getting from Griffith a written statement promising that he would accept a commission to regulate the boundary between the two states should Ulster refuse to join an all-Ireland parliament. As Griffith reported to de Valera, this was but a 'tactical manoeuvre' to put the blame for any break in the talks on Ulster.

At the end of the negotiations, with the Irish delegates still pressing for unity, this scrap of paper was triumphantly produced by Lloyd George. He challenged Griffith with having given his word 'not to let him down'.

'I have never let a man down in my whole life and I never will,' replied Griffith, who now found his 'tactical manoeuvre' had been cleverly used to trap him.

Lloyd George was now determined to force the issue. He offered one big concession: the new state would have its own independent monetary system. Then, speaking with all the solemnity and force he could muster, he informed the delegates that they must sign the articles of agreement that very day or there would be 'immediate and terrible war'. All the delegates must sign. He who refused must bear the responsibility for the war. The delegation had until ten o'clock to make a decision.

Griffith and Collins were prepared to sign, convinced that better terms could not be had. They probably felt that the president would support their action, since there seemed so little difference between the draft Treaty and the document they were being asked to sign.

They were mistaken in this, but had they not urged the president to be ready to come over to London?

Duggan was satisfied to follow the example of Griffith and Collins. Gavan Duffy and Barton were against signing. In the end, they gave in under pressure.

The document which they signed was entitled 'Articles of Agreement for a Treaty between Great Britain and Ireland, December 6, 1921'. It was not in itself the Treaty. It would not become law until it was passed by the elected representatives of both countries. In theory, therefore, it could be argued that nothing was lost – yet.

It was just three years since Michael Collins had written an old Irish saying in a young girl's autograph book: *Seachain éadan tairbh, drannadh madra deireadh chapaill agus gáire Shasanaigh* (Beware of the bull's forehead, the snarling of a dog, the hind-part of a horse and the laugh of an Englishman). He was very upset when the president appointed him a member of the team which was to negotiate a treaty with the British government.

'I should not have been asked to go,' he said to Batt O'Connor. 'It is a mistake to send me. De Valera should go. Whoever heard of the soldier who fought the enemy in the field being sent to negotiate the peace? I am being put in an impossible position. I fought hard against my selection,' he cried out. 'De Valera pressed me. For no other man living would I have consented.'

The wisdom of his nomination seems questionable today. If the war had been resumed, Collins could not have hoped to escape capture and death once his appearance was known to the enemy. But this would not have worried him so much had he not felt that he was the wrong person for the task. Negotiations belonged to politicians and he was not a politician.

That he was being sent to negotiate for

something less than he had been fighting for was a further cause of worry to him. Like the rest of the cabinet, he knew that it would not be possible to bring back the republic for which they had all been working and fighting.

The rank and file in the movement had no knowledge of this. Collins saw that there would be trouble. To the members of Dáil Éireann he said: 'I go in the spirit of a soldier who acts against his judgment at the orders of a superior officer.'

During the negotiations, the delegation stayed at 22 Hans Place. The offices were in 15 Cadogan Gardens where, for business reasons, Collins found it convenient to stay. With him went Ned Broy, the former detective, who had lately been released from detention in Arbour Hill Barracks.

It was noticed that Collins slipped out quietly each morning during his stay and returned just in time for breakfast. Fearing for his safety, Broy decided to follow him. He was perhaps a little surprised to discover that Michael was going to hear eight o'clock Mass in Brompton Oratory.

By common consent, the delegates kept their social life in London to a minimum. Invitations from English people they did not accept. They did, however, visit the houses of sympathisers. In this way, Collins made the acquaintance of many well-known figures in artistic and literary circles. To his acquaintance with Sir John Lavery, the Belfast painter, and his wife, we are indebted for the fine painting of his lying in state. Sir James Barrie was charmed by him. Apart from these friends, Collins led a quiet life. He visited his sister Johanna frequently.

Once again, Griffith and Collins were working together in the absence of the president. Lloyd George and the English politicians soon saw that they were the 'strong men' of the Irish delegation. Whatever Griffith and

Collins agreed upon, the rest would follow. So the Welshman reasoned. He therefore concentrated all his efforts on them. Almost unknown to themselves, a division of opinion now appeared among the Irishmen. Barton and Gavan Duffy were both somewhat out of touch with the realities of the situation at home – Barton owing to long imprisonment, and Gavan Duffy owing to absence abroad. Both were opposed to signing. Griffith and Collins were under no illusion about Ireland's ability to continue the fight with much chance of success. Collins especially knew that the British had been forced to the conference table as much by the pressure of public opinion abroad as by Sinn Féin's military successes.

To him and to Griffith, the terms offered by the British gave more than any Irishmen before them had been offered before 1916. After 1916 and during the War of Independence, however, hopes had risen so high that the Treaty seemed a step back rather than a step forward. Any advantages it contained faded away before Article 4, which required the members of Dáil Éireann to swear allegiance to the British crown. How could those who had already sworn allegiance to the republic violate their oath by taking one to the British king?

Collins himself was aware of this contradiction and the falseness of his own position in the matter. He finally decided to sign, feeling that the final responsibility for acceptance or rejection lay with the elected representatives of the people of Ireland.

The Articles of Agreement were signed at 2.20 on the morning of Tuesday 6 December 1921.

'I have signed my own death warrant,' was Collins's gloomy comment.

Lloyd George had solved his problem. By an unworthy trick, he had trapped Griffith into giving in on Ulster. But the Irish problem was not solved. For all his cleverness,

Lloyd George's solution was not a lasting one. Less than fifty years later, it was to be the cause of further bloodshed and loss of life among Irish and British alike.

THE GREAT DEBATE

THE TRAGIC EVENTS which Michael Collins foresaw were now about to unfold. The unity that had held the country firm in the face of the enemy's worst attacks was now breaking. Two opposing 'sides' were slowly emerging: those who accepted the Treaty and those who rejected it.

Collins was disappointed to learn that the president would not be recommending acceptance at the forthcoming Dáil debate on the Treaty. De Valera could not accept the terms of the proposed Treaty. His own draft treaty represented the most he would concede to the British. He now proposed an alternative.

Meanwhile, from towns and villages and remote country areas, the deputies flocked to the assembled Dáil on 14 December 1921. The occasion was an historic one, reminiscent of the last meeting of Grattan's Parliament in 1800. The meeting was held in the council chamber of the university building in Earlsfort Terrace, Dublin. Reporters of the world's leading newspapers were present. So, too, were members of the public, who crowded the visitors' section. The tension was great even before the debate itself started.

One eyewitness called the Treaty debate the 'greatest Niagara of continuous eloquence in Irish history'. There was much oratory and many moving professions of faith in Ireland, the Republic and its representatives, depending on the side taken by the speakers. Many spoke at great length; Mary MacSwiney, sister of the martyred lord mayor of Cork, spoke for two-and-a-half hours, hardly glancing at her notes. Others spoke little. There was anger, sorrow and laughter, too. Many of the speeches were irrelevant to the main issue. Sometimes it seemed as though the issue was not quite clear: was it a choice between the Treaty and war, or between an independent republic and a British dominion? Or was it between the Treaty and the president's alternative? Or between two forms of association with the British Empire?

Descriptions of the speakers have come down to us. There was Madame Markievicz in a white blouse and a black fur, shaking hands with visitors; Seán MacEoin in a tweed suit; Pádraic Ó Maille of Connemara, whose fine Irish brought a breath of the west into the assembly.

An eyewitness described the chief actors in the drama: 'Messrs Éamon de Valera, Austin Stack and Erskine Childers are seated together. Mr de Valera, with his hand to his mouth, looks absorbed. The minister for home affairs wears that stern look which rarely leaves his face. Erskine Childers is reflective in that pale, rather white, and keenly cold way of his. The ladies, in deep black, seem sombre. Michael Collins, clean-shaven, looks perfectly fit and in perfect good humour.'

Éamon de Valera spoke. 'His blinding sincerity so impresses you that you find yourself listening dazzled and profoundly moved. Every word came with rugged clearness. Here was no faltering or no hesitation.'

Michael Collins spoke. 'He spoke passionately, eagerly, pervadingly. He had his manuscript before him. He rarely consulted it. He preferred to rely on his intuition – on the unfailing national power of the Irishman to move, rouse and convince his hearers. Now and again he felt his smooth chin. He tossed his black hair with his hands. He rummaged among his documents … he stands now upright, now bent, now calm, and now quivering with emotion. On a previous occasion, I said that Michael Collins spoke slowly. He does – until he is aroused. Then the words come in a ceaseless stream.'

Collins defended the actions of the delegates, reminding his hearers: '… if we all stood on the recognition of the Irish Republic, as a prelude to any conference, we could easily have said so, and there would be no conference … it was the acceptance of the invitation that formed the compromise. I was sent there to form that adaptation, to bear the brunt of it. Now, as one of the signatories of the document, I naturally recommend its acceptance. I do not recommend it for more than it is. Equally I do not recommend it for less than it is. In my opinion it gives us freedom, not the ultimate freedom that all nations desire and develop to, but the freedom to achieve it.'

It was characteristic of him that at no stage did he shirk responsibility for his actions, and that his thoughts were already busy with the task of nation-building. The withdrawal of the British Army and administration would give Ireland control of her own affairs. 'Are we never going to stand on our own feet?' he asked.

This is how one account describes the

climax to his speech: From slow, measured tones, his speech mounted until it reached a crescendo of anger and indignation.

'I have not said a harsh word about anybody, yet I have been called a traitor. Well, let the Irish people decide whether I am or not.'

De Valera, with lightning rapidity, jerked out the words, 'By whom?'

Collins continued speaking: 'If there are men who act towards me as a traitor I am prepared to meet them anywhere, any time, now as in the past.'

It was a challenge – not uttered with provocative emphasis, but with deep feeling. Members and deputies became a little restless. Then, with astounding rapidity, the mercury fell.

In almost ordinary tones, but with the emphatic note never absent, Michael Collins placed his cards on the table. 'Ireland has full liberty to accept or reject. I signed and I recommended. That is all. If the Dáil does not accept, I am relieved of all responsibility. I fall into the ranks.'

The words had a soothing effect.

The debate continued. One deputy, an opponent of the Treaty, ranged from *Webster's Dictionary* to the Bible in his speech. Pádraic Ó Maille reminded his listeners that the impetuosity of the youthful Aodh Rua Ó Domhnaill had lost the day at Kinsale for the older and more wily Aodh Ó Neill. A female deputy could not accept the Treaty on account of the oath to the British king, yet, she said, she wanted peace. A youthful deputy from Mayo explained that he could not accept the Treaty as it did not secure the unity of Ireland; he saw little prospect of a united Ireland in the future. It was a Tipperary deputy who uttered the words, 'Damn the Treaty and what about the consequences!'

'Hands off the Republic!' said another, with commendable brevity.

Looking back, many will agree with the

remarks made by Dr McCartan, a strong republican:

> *The people elected us to direct the destinies of Ireland at this period, and we elected a Cabinet. I submit it was their duty to lead us, the rank and file, in the best possible way. I submit that they have failed one and all. They are divided; we are therefore divided. I submit it is a mock division and I submit the whole Cabinet were equally responsible for the position in which we find ourselves today.*

In the New Year, Collins seems to have lost patience, for he referred to some of his opponents as 'bullies'. The Ceann Comhairle (as the chairperson of the Dáil is called) told him he must withdraw the term.

He paused. He sought inspiration in the documents before him. Again, there was tense silence. Anxiety was written on every countenance. Would Michael refuse to withdraw?

Would there be a scene? Was there material for a fatal rupture if the minister of finance remained obstinate?

Almost a minute passed. And still not a word.

Then, slowly, deliberately, and with emphasis, Michael Collins spoke: 'I can withdraw the term – but the spoken word cannot be recalled.' And with schoolboyish naivety, Michael looked at the Ceann Comhairle, and added, 'Is that right, sir?'

There was laughter.

Those who bore a grudge against Collins now vented their feelings in bitter personal attacks on him. One speaker objected to the publicity accorded him by the press, and took exception to Griffith's reference to him as 'the man who won the war'.

Griffith answered with fire:

I said it and I say it again; he was the man who made the situation; he was the man,

*and nobody knows better than I do, how,
during a year and a half, he worked from
six in the morning until two next morning.
He was the man whose matchless energy,
whose indomitable will, carried Ireland
through the terrible crisis; and though I have
not now, and never had, an ambition about
either political affairs or history, if my name
is to go down in history, I want it associated
with the name of Michael Collins.*

And so the debate continued until 7 January
1922, when the Treaty was put to the vote.
The result was sixty-four in favour and fifty-
seven against.

Collins was on his feet immediately, asking
for permission to speak. Having obtained it,
he made a speech that breathed his passion-
ate concern for Ireland and her people, his
generosity to his opponents, and his complete
selflessness. To those who voted against the
Treaty, he said: 'I do not regard the passing of

this thing as being any kind of triumph over the other side. I will do my best in the future, as I have done in the past, for the nation.'

Having pointed out the dangers for the country of the transitional period, he suggested the appointment of a joint committee composed of members from both sides to take over the machinery of government from the British. In conclusion, he said with feeling:

I only want to say this to the people who are against us – and there are good people against us – so far as I am concerned this is not a question of politics, nor never has been. I make the promise publicly to the Irish nation that I will do my best, and though some people here have said hard things of me, I would not stand things like that said about the other side. I have just as high a regard for some of them, and am prepared to do as much for them now, as always. The

President knows how I tried to do my best for him.

The president indicated his agreement. Michael looked at him, and turning to the assembly said: 'Well, he has exactly the same position in my heart now as he always had.'

The president rose to close the meeting. In a broken voice, de Valera appealed for unity. The eyes of the world were on them now. Then he broke down and wept.

The cheers, mingled with boos, of the waiting crowds gathered outside could now be heard in the chamber.

The decision taken on that historic day was to bring tragedy to some and sorrow to all.

THE HERO LIGHT

ON 16 JANUARY 1922 Dublin Castle – the symbol of foreign domination – was handed over to the young man who had destroyed its power: Michael Collins, now head of the Provisional Government.

The occasion was marred by the bitter divisions around him. If only a united Ireland and a united people could have shared the joy of the moment! But it was not to be.

The chief actors in the events of the next few months seem to have been aware of the dangers of civil war. When finally it broke out, it was not for lack of efforts to prevent it. Looking back, it seems as though their efforts were doomed from the first.

In no one was this so apparent as in Collins. The most loyal and generous of men, he now found ranged against him his old friends: de Valera, Harry Boland and Rory

O'Connor, to name but a few. The attacks of his enemies continued. He wrote sadly: 'They are all knifing me now.'

As both sides drifted even further apart, Collins faced the problems of trying to reconcile loyalty to his friends with the responsibilities of his position. His efforts at conciliation were looked on with suspicion by the British government.

The climax was reached in April when Rory O'Connor, Liam Mellows and a group of anti-Treaty members of the IRA seized and occupied the Four Courts. Firm in their belief that the Dáil had no right to accept the Treaty, they recognised no political organisation. However, they were not interfered with until June.

The situation in the north-east of the country had also grown worse. There had been attacks by Orange elements on the nationalist population. Collins sent protest after protest to the British government. He even got in touch with Liam Lynch, who, though an opponent of the Treaty, was prepared to collaborate with the army of the Provisional Government in defending the northern nationalists. It was to the credit of both men that they were prepared to cooperate for Ireland's sake, despite political differences.

On 16 June an election was held. Of the Sinn Féin members elected, fifty-eight supported the Treaty and thirty-six opposed it. It looked as though popular support was behind the government. Then the blow fell.

Sir Henry Wilson, whose wild threats were thought by many to be responsible for the northern attacks, was assassinated in London by two Irishmen. The British government now had a pretext for forcing the Provisional Government to move against the 'rebels' in the Four Courts. An ultimatum was issued by Winston Churchill: if the Provisional Government would not act, the British government would consider the Treaty broken and take matters into its own hands. It seemed there was nothing the Provisional Government could do but issue an ultimatum in its turn to the Four Courts garrison. This was ignored and so the attack on the Four Courts began. It lasted three days before the garrison surrendered unconditionally. But the fight continued in the O'Connell Street area, where the anti-Treaty republicans had barricaded themselves into hotels and offices. It was there that Cathal Brugha, the uncompromising republican, chose death rather than surrender.

From then on, disaster followed disaster: Harry Boland – Collins's close friend of happier days – was shot and mortally wounded by government troops. A fortnight later Arthur Griffith, physically worn out by strain and sorrow, died.

Now it was Collins's turn. Death came to him in his own country of West Cork, amidst his own people. What the English had failed to do was to be done by his own countrymen.

He was now commander-in-chief of the army – a post that gave more scope to his organisational talents. He started on a tour of inspection of the south of Ireland, in the course of which he resolved to try to meet Liam Lynch and, with his help, endeavour to bring the fighting to an end. So his last journey was in quest of peace.

On the morning of Tuesday 22 August 1922, Collins and a small party set out for Bandon. From there they went to Clonakilty and Sam's Cross, where the Collins family gathered to receive him. To his brother Johnny he confided that he had come south to try to find a way of ending the civil war.

As dusk was falling, the party drove back towards Cork. As they came up to the crossroads at Béal na mBláth, they unexpectedly encountered a group of republicans, and in the exchanges that followed, the commander-in-chief was mortally wounded.

Michael Collins had passed into history.

The whole of Ireland mourned the passing of Michael Collins. Like Eoghan Rua Ó Neill, his death came at a crucial time in the history of his people. Had he lived, it is just possible that the worst of the civil war might have been averted. His death killed any hope that peace would prevail.

Perhaps they were right who believed that God in His goodness had spared him a future of strife and bitterness. He died the death of a soldier, as he would have wished.

The most fitting tribute came from the pen of that courageous defender of Irish patriots, George Bernard Shaw. To Collins's sister Johanna, he wrote:

> *Don't let them make you miserable about it: how could a born soldier die better than at the victorious end of a good fight, falling to the shot of another Irishman – a damned fool, but all the same an Irishman*

who thought he was fighting for Ireland; 'A Roman to a Roman?' I met Michael for the first and last time on Saturday last, and am very glad I did. I rejoice in his memory and will not be so disloyal to it as to snivel over his valiant death. So tear up your mourning and hang up your brightest colours in his honour; and let us all praise God that he had not to die in a snuffy bed of a trumpery cough, weakened by age and saddened by the disappointments that would have attended his work had he lived.